Introduction

The goal of this book is to introduce the Tamil script to a child who is familiar with the English language. The script is taught through a number of puzzles and activities which when completed provide familiarity with the alphabet.

For each letter in the Tamil alphabet, different types of activity sheets are provided. They include coloring in the letter, coloring the picture of an object that begins with the letter, trying to find the letter in a maze and finding letters in figures. As the child solves the puzzles, he/she gains familiarity with the letter, and learns to recognize its shape.

A sequence of fading outlines is included for each letter. The child can trace those letters and try to make them on his or her own as well.

The book also explains the concept of conjugations of vowels and consonants and has a set of activities and puzzles that enable children to learn the alphabet with conjugated letters while having fun at the same time.

All the activities are introduced by Sir, the cute dog who will teach Tamil to all.

Hand over a set of crayons to your child with this book and see how it turns learning Tamil into an enjoyable game.

Acknowledgements:
Many thanks to my Tamil friends Lakshmi Kishore and Senthil Nathan for reviewing this book.

Chanda Books
Email: chandabooks@optonline.net
Web: http://www.chandabooks.com

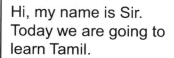

Hi, my name is Sir. Today we are going to learn Tamil.

There are thirty-six(36) letters or characters in the Tamil alphabet. Each letter represents one sound. The sounds are divided into two types, just like English: vowels and consonants.

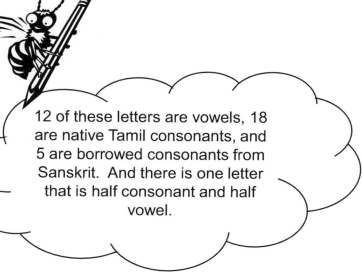

12 of these letters are vowels, 18 are native Tamil consonants, and 5 are borrowed consonants from Sanskrit. And there is one letter that is half consonant and half vowel.

Tamil Alphabet

Vowels (உயிரெழுத்து)
அ ஆ இ ஈ உ ஊ
எ ஏ ஐ ஒ ஓ ஔ

Hybrid (அலியெழுத்து)
ஃ

Consonants (மெய்யெழுத்து)
க ங ச ஞ ட ண
த ந ப ம ய ர
ல வ ழ ள ற ன

Grantha Letters (கிரந்த)
ஜ ஷ ஸ ஹ க்ஷ

Pronunciation Rules

The pronunciation of letters in Tamil depends on the position of the letter in the word. The following is a simplified set of rules to help a beginner.

The following letters change their sounds depending on their position in the word: க,ச,ட,த,ப

க: In beginning of a word, or when it occurs adjacent to letters க,ச,ட,த,ப or ற, is pronounced like the first syllable (co) in <u>co</u>me. When it occurs in a word next to ந், ஞ,ண,ம or ன, it is pronounced like the first syllable (g) of <u>g</u>um. When it occurs between two vowels or after ர் and ய் it is pronounced like first syllable (h) of <u>h</u>um.

ச: is usually pronounced like first syllable (ch) of <u>ch</u>urch. When it occurs in a word next to ந், ஞ,ண,ம or ன, is pronounced like first syllable (j) of <u>j</u>ug. When it occurs between two vowels, it is pronounced like first syllable (s) of <u>s</u>un. In words of Sanskrit origins, it is also pronounced like first syllable (s) of <u>s</u>un in initial position.

ட: is usually pronounced like first syllable (t) of <u>t</u>ub. When it occurs in a word after ந், ஞ,ண,ம or ன, or between two vowels, it is pronounced like second syllable (th) of fa<u>th</u>er.

த: Is usually pronounced like first syllable (th) in <u>th</u>ug. When it occurs in a word next to ந், ஞ,ண,ம or ன, or in between vowels, it is pronounced like first syllable (dh) of <u>dh</u>arma.

ப: is usually pronounced like first syllable (p) of <u>p</u>ub. When it occurs in a word after ந், ஞ,ண,ம or ன, or between two vowels, it is pronounced like first syllable (b) of <u>b</u>us.

For a more comprehensive set of nuances and rules related to Tamil pronunciation, please consult a Tamil Grammar book.

We will start by learning the vowels of Tamil.

There are 12 vowels in the Tamil alphabet.

Tamil Vowels

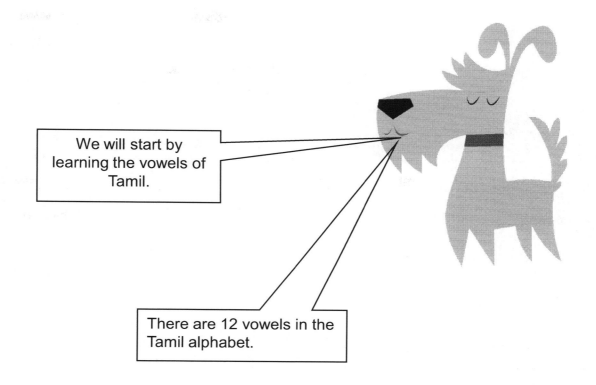

The vowel sounds can be made on their own, but consonants always need the help of a vowel to make a sound.

அ

The first vowel in Tamil is the letter அ. It makes the sound of first a in **a**way.

Color me blue

Color me red

One word beginning with அ is அணில் (anil) or squirrel. Color this அணில்.

Another word beginning with அ is அமெரிக்கா, which is America written in Tamil. Color this map of America. If you live in USA, mark your city on this map.

BALTIM-ORE

Try making the letter அ on your own.

அ

Amit Rabbit is only allowed to hop onto adjacent stones that are marked with the letter அ. Can you find a way for Amit to reach a carrot? Color all the stones Amit will need to jump on his way blue.

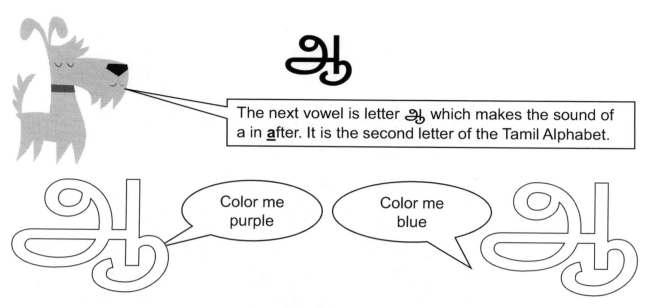

ஆ

The next vowel is letter ஆ which makes the sound of a in **a**fter. It is the second letter of the Tamil Alphabet.

Color me purple

Color me blue

One word beginning with ஆ is ஆடு (aadu) or goat. Color this picture of a goat.

Another word beginning with ஆ is ஆணி (aani) or nail. Color these nails in metallic gray or your choice of colors.

Try making the letter ஆ on your own.

Only some of the pictures shown here begin with ஆ .
Can you circle the pictures that begin with it?

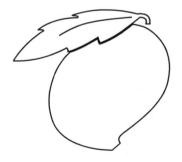

List of Words				
ஆடு (aadu)	goat		ஆமை (aamai)	turtle
கப்பல் (kappal)	ship		ஆஸ்பத்திரி (aaspatthiri)	hospital
தாமரை(thaamarai)	lotus		மாம்பழம் (maampazham)	mango

Another vowel is இ, which makes the sound of i in **it**. It is the third letter in the Tamil Alphabet.

Color me purple

Color me blue

One word beginning with இ is இலை (ilai) or leaf. Color this leaf green.

Another word beginning with இ is இட்லி (idli) which we all like to eat. Color this yummy bunch of idlis.

Try making the letter இ on your own.

Some of the apples on this page are of type இ and others are of different types. Can you circle and color all the apples of type இ?

ஈ

One more vowel is the letter ஈ that makes the sound of ee in **ee**l.

Color me red

Color me green

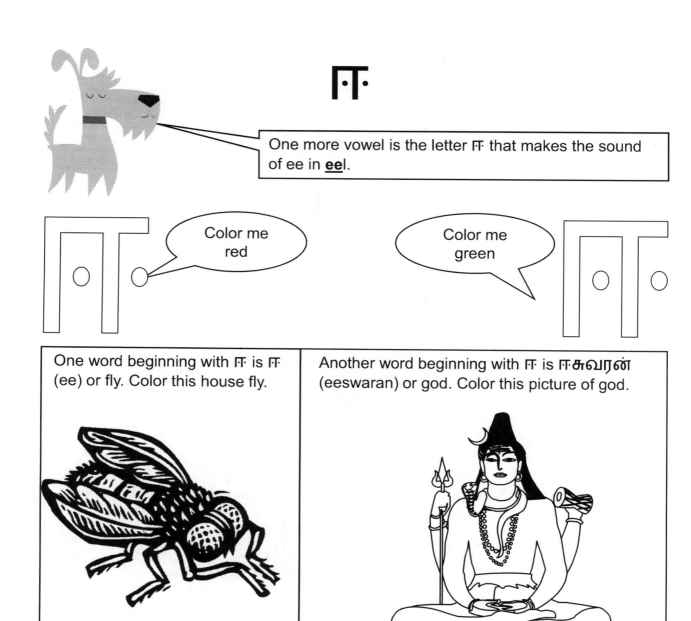

One word beginning with ஈ is ஈ (ee) or fly. Color this house fly.

Another word beginning with ஈ is ஈசுவரன் (eeswaran) or god. Color this picture of god.

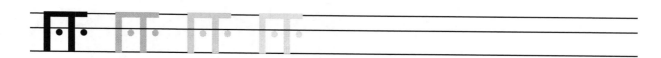

Try making the letter ஈ on your own.

ஈ

Golu Elephant is only allowed to walk on boxes that are marked ஈ. He can only move between adjacent boxes left/right or up/down. Can you find a way for Golu to reach the bananas?

ஈ	ஈ	ல	வ	ஈ	வ	ஈ	ஈ	ஈ	ஈ	ர
ஜ	ஈ	ஈ	ல	ஈ	ஈ	ஈ	வ	வ	க	க
ஈ	ஈ	ம	ஈ	ஈ	வ	ஈ	ர	ஈ	க	ஈ
வ	ஈ	ஈ	ஈ	ஈ	ப	ஈ	ஈ	ஈ	ஈ	ஈ
ம	ப	இ	அ	இ	ர	ம	க	வ	ஈ	ப
ஈ	ஈ	ஈ	ஈ	ஜ	ஈ	ஈ	ஈ	வ	ஈ	ல
ந	வ	ஜ	வ	ப	ஈ	வ	ஈ	ம	ஈ	ஈ
ப	ல	ர	ஈ	ஈ	ஈ	வ	ஈ	ஈ	ஈ	ஈ
ஈ	ஈ	ஈ	ஈ	வ	ஈ	ல	அ	வ	ஜ	உ

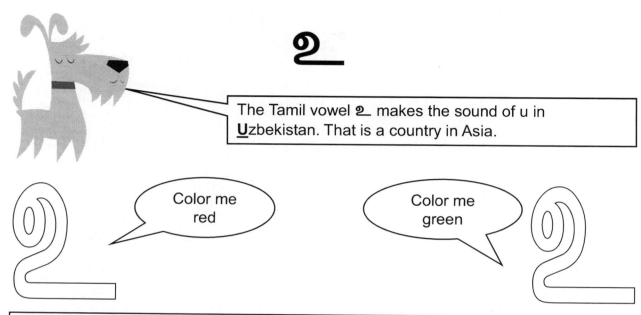

The Tamil vowel உ makes the sound of u in **U**zbekistan. That is a country in Asia.

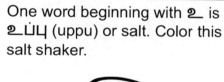

Color me red

Color me green

One word beginning with உ is உப்பு (uppu) or salt. Color this salt shaker.

Another word beginning with உ is உலகம் (ulakam) or the world. Color the oceans of this world blue and continents brown.

Try making the letter உ on your own.

௨

Santa knows that only the stockings marked with the letter ௨ belong to kids who have been nice. He will only fill those stockings with gifts. Can you color the stockings Santa will fill red?

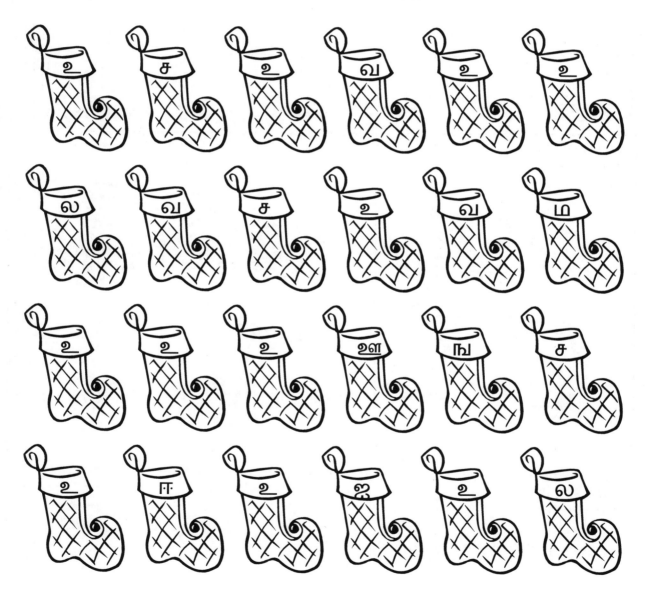

ஊ

The Tamil letter ஊ makes the sound of oo in **oo**h.

Color me red

Color me green

One word beginning with ஊ is ஊசி (oosi) or needle. Color this need and its thread.

Another word beginning with ஊ is ஊஞ்சல் (oonjal) or swing. Color this swing in your favorite colors.

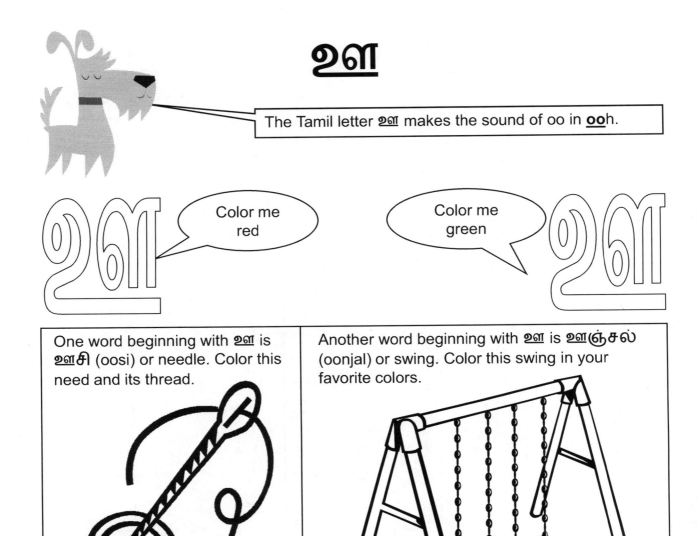

ஊ ஊ ஊ ஊ

Try making the letter ஊ on your own.

உள

My alphabet soup has quite a few letters and I have lost track of the number of உள in my soup. Can you find out how many உள are in my bowl of soup?

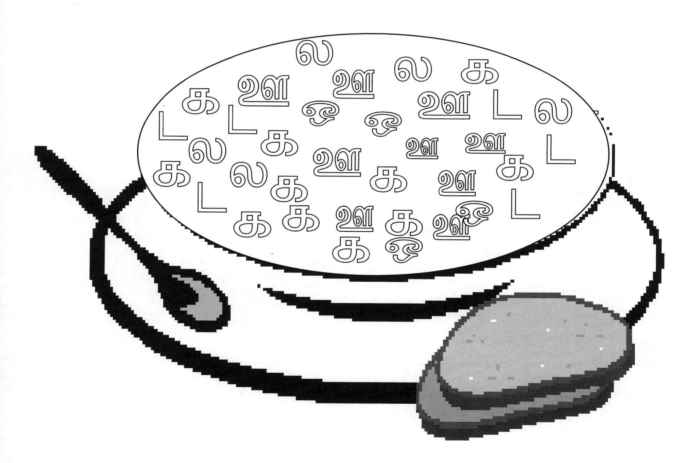

எ

The Tamil letter எ makes the sound of ey in h**ey**.

Color me red

Color me green

One word beginning with எ is எலி (eyli) or rat. Color this rat brown.

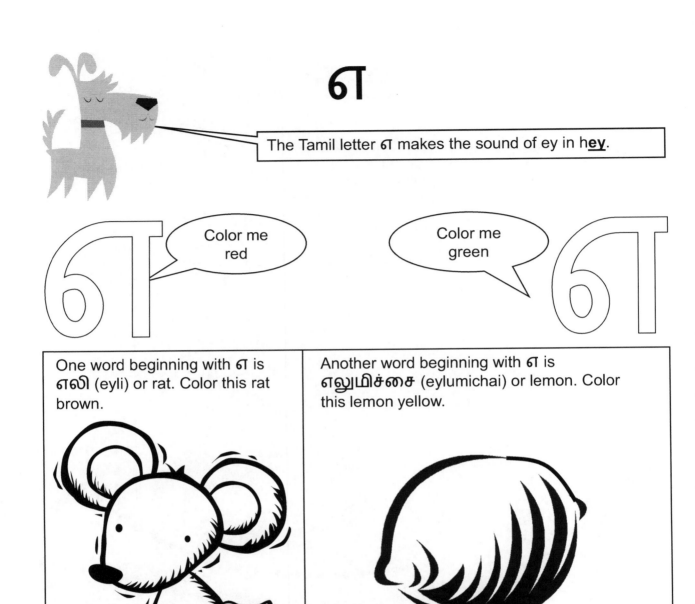

Another word beginning with எ is எலுமிச்சை (eylumichai) or lemon. Color this lemon yellow.

Try making the letter எ on your own.

எ

Eyli the Mouse is only allowed to hop onto adjacent hexagons that are marked எ. Can you find a way for Eyli to reach a piece of cheese? Which cheese piece does he get to eat?

Answer: He reaches cheese piece 1

ஏ

The Tamil letter ஏ makes the sound of a in **a**te.

Color me red

Color me green

One word beginning with ஏ is ஏணி (ayni) or ladder. Color this ladder in your choice of colors.

Another word beginning with ஏ is ஏழு (ayzhu) or the number 7. Color this number 7.

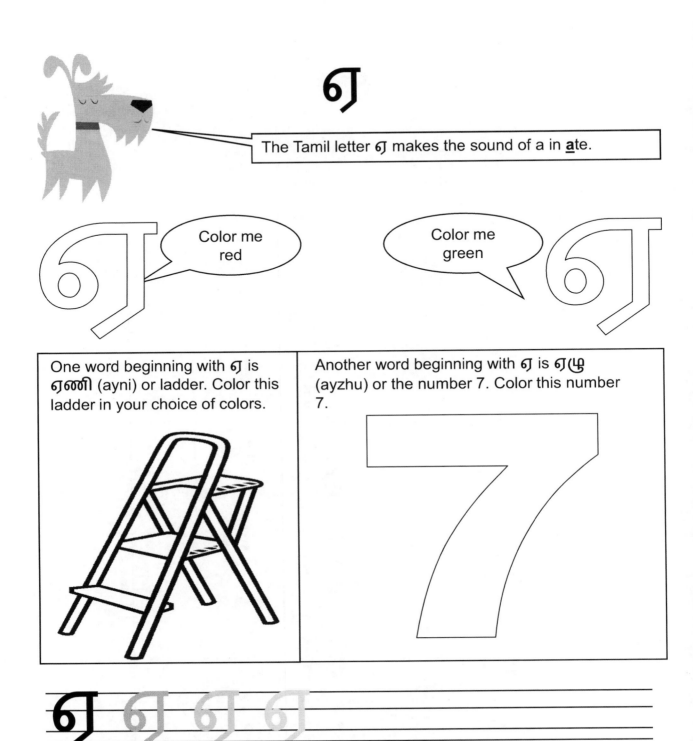

Try making the letter ஏ on your own.

ஏ

My alphabet soup has quite a few letters and I have lost track of the number of ஏ in my soup. Can you find out how many ஏ are in my bowl of soup?

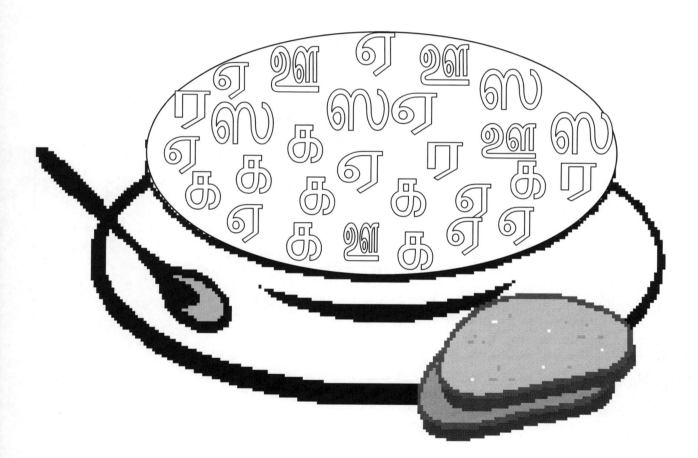

ஐ

The Tamil letter ஐ makes the sound of eye in **eye**.

Color me red

Color me green

One word beginning with ஐ is ஐந்து (eyenthu) or the number 5. Paint this number red.

Another word beginning with ஐ is ஐங்கோணம் (eyeingakonam) which means a pentagon. Color this pentagon in your favorite color.

Try making the letter ஐ on your own.

Some of the toffees on this page are of type ஐ and others are of different types. Can you circle and color all the toffees of type ஐ?

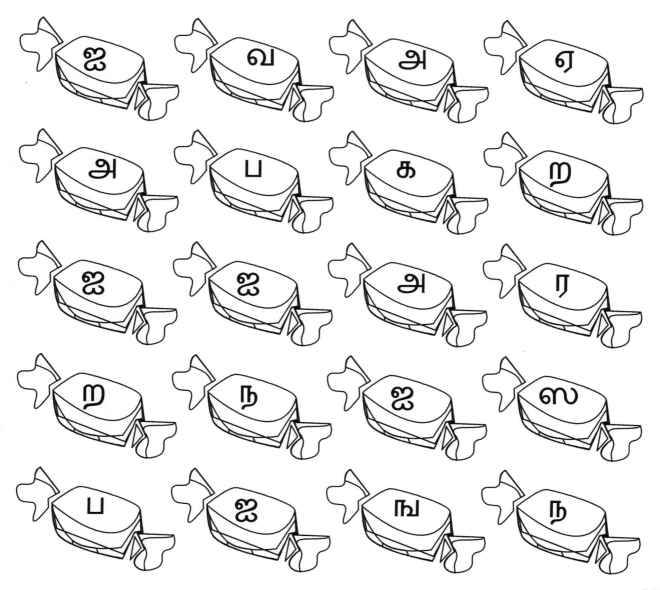

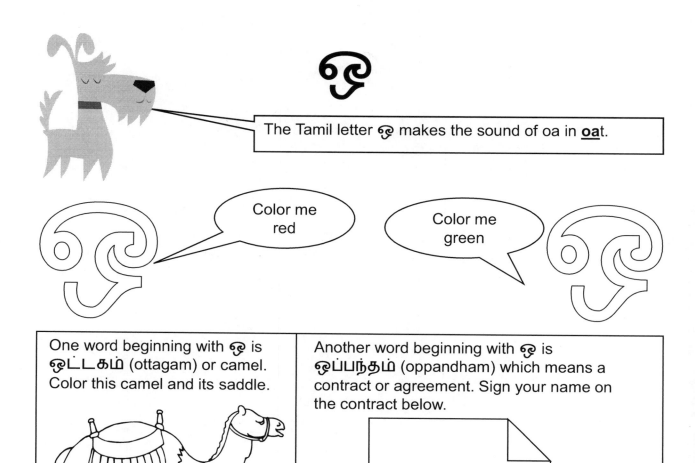

The Tamil letter ஓ makes the sound of oa in **oa**t.

Color me red

Color me green

One word beginning with ஓ is ஓட்டகம் (ottagam) or camel. Color this camel and its saddle.

Another word beginning with ஓ is ஓப்பந்தம் (oppandham) which means a contract or agreement. Sign your name on the contract below.

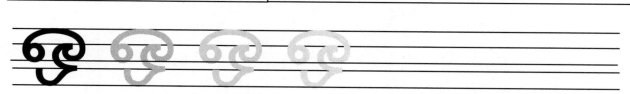

Try making the letter ஓ on your own.

Golu Elephant is only allowed to walk on boxes that are marked ஒ. He can only move between adjacent boxes left/right or up/down. Can you find a way for Golu to reach the bananas?

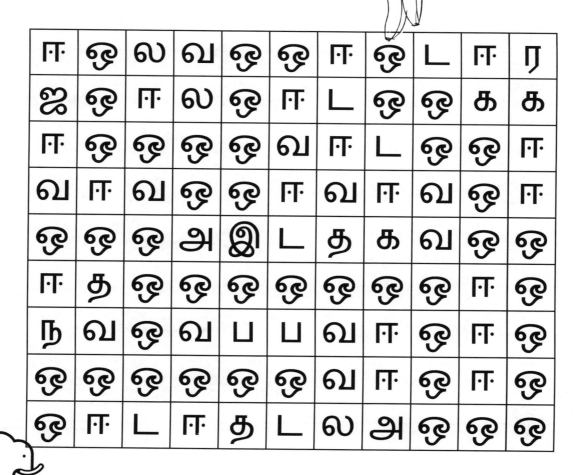

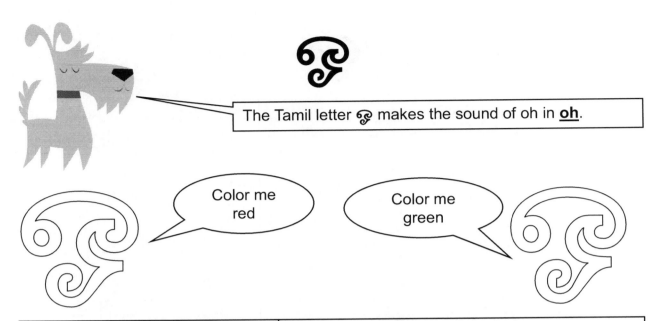

The Tamil letter ஓ makes the sound of oh in **oh**.

Color me red

Color me green

One word beginning with ஓ is ஓங்காரம் (omkaram) or the letter om. Color this letter.

Another word beginning with ஓ is ஓட்டப்பம் (ottappam) which is a pancake type dish. Color this ottappam a tasty brown.

Try making the letter ஓ on your own.

Eyli the Mouse is only allowed to hop onto adjacent hexagons that are marked ஒ. Can you find a way for Eyli to reach a piece of cheese? Which cheese piece does he get to eat?

Answer: He reaches cheese piece3

ஒள

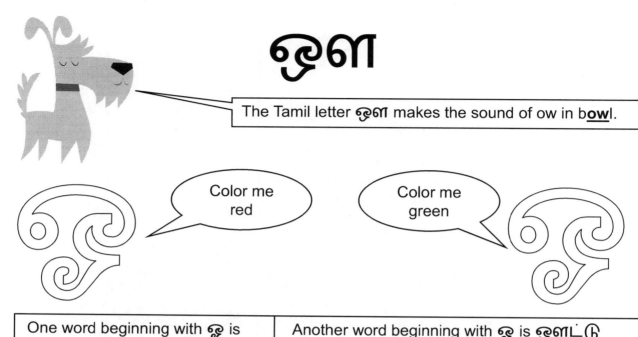

The Tamil letter ஒள makes the sound of ow in b**ow**l.

Color me red

Color me green

One word beginning with ஒ is ஒளடதம் (owtatum) or medicine. Color this medicine bottle.

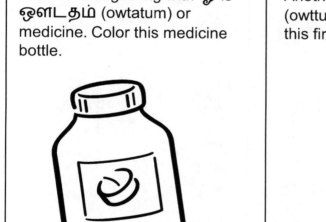

Another word beginning with ஒ is ஒளட்டு (owttu) which is a type of firecracker. Color this firecracker.

Try making the letter ஒள on your own.

ஒள

Some of the apples on this page are of type ஒள and others are of different types. Can you circle and color all the apples of type ஒள ?

There are 18 native consonants in Tamil. Each consonant has one or more sounds, the sound depending on its position in the word.

Did I tell you that consonants sound usually come with a vowel. When they are without a vowel, a small dot is put on top of them.

Tamil Consonants

க ங ச ஞ ட ண
த ந ப ம ய ர
ல வ ழ ள ற ன

க

The Tamil letter க normally makes the sound of co in **co**me. But in some other cases, it makes the sound of gu in **gu**m.

Color me red

Color me green

One word beginning with க is கரடி (karadi) or bear. Color this bear brown.

Another word beginning with க is கடலை (kadalai) which means peanuts. Color this group of peanuts.

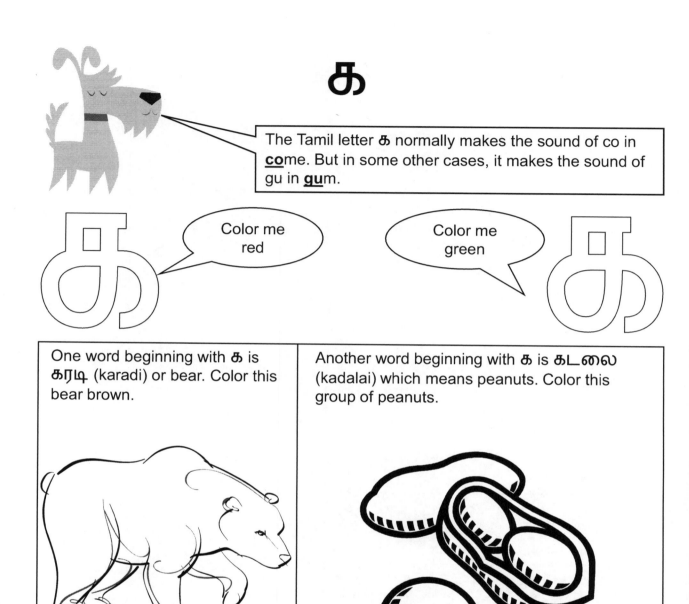

க க க க

Try making the letter க on your own.

க

Only some of the pictures shown here begin with க .
Can you circle those pictures that begin with it?
Color those pictures green.

List of Words			
ஆமை (aamai)	turtle	கழுதை (kaluthai)	donkey
கப்பல் (kappal)	ship	பேனா (penaa)	pen
கமலம்(kamalam)	lotus	பந்து (pandhu)	ball

ங

The Tamil letter ங makes the sound of ngh in u**ngh**. It is more common to find words that have it in the middle.

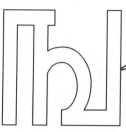

Color me red

Color me green

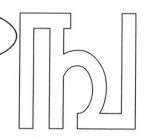

One word containing ங is சிங்கம் (singam) or lion. Color this lion in ferocious colors.

Another word containing ங is குரங்கு (kurangu) which means a monkey. Color this monkey.

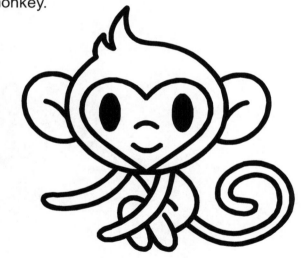

ங ங ங ங

Try making the letter ங on your own.

ங

Eyli the Mouse is only allowed to hop onto adjacent hexagons that are marked ங. Can you find a way for Eyli to reach a piece of cheese. Which cheese piece does he get to eat?

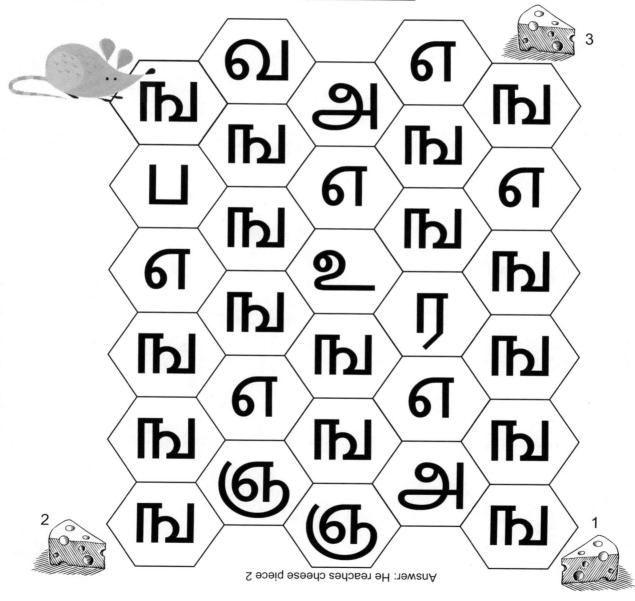

Answer: He reaches cheese piece 2

ச

The Tamil letter ச usually makes the sound of ch in **ch**urch. In words borrowed from Sanskrit, it makes the sound of s in **su**n. Sometimes, it makes the sound of j in **ju**g.

Color me red

Color me green

One word beginning with சis சக்கரம் (chakkaram) or wheel. Color this wheel

Another word beginning with சis சர்க்கரை (sarkkarai) or sugar. Color this bag of sugar.

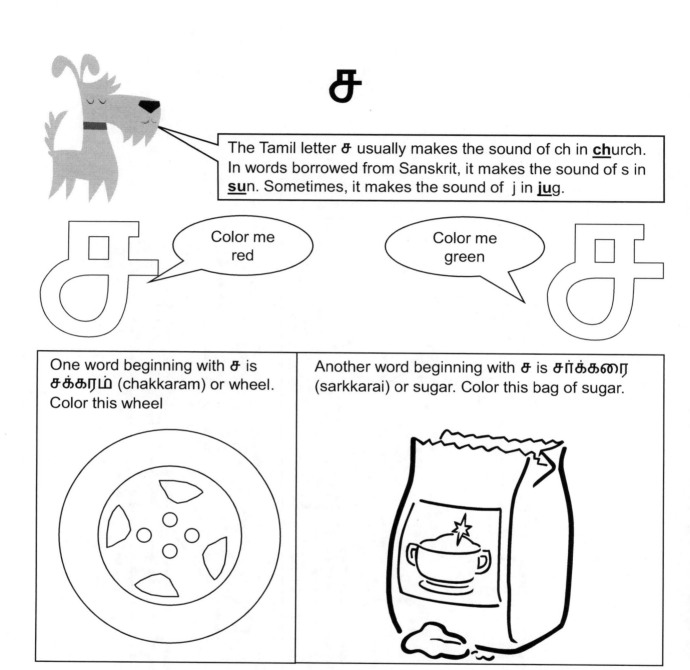

Try making the letter சon your own.

ச

Only some of the pictures shown here begin with ச .
Can you circle those pictures that begin with it?
Color those pictures green.

List of Words			
சாவி (saavi)	key	சூரியன் (suriyan)	Sun
கப்பல் (kappal)	ship	சாப்பாடு (saapadu)	meal
சந்திரன்(chandhiran)	moon	பந்து (pandhu)	ball

ங

The Tamil letter ங makes the sound of ngha. It is usually found in the middle of words, and not in beginning.

Color me red

Color me green

One word containing ங is பஞ்சி (panji) or cotton. Color this cotton ball.

Another word containing ங is அஞ்சலி (anjali) which means folding hands in prayer. Color this person.

ங ங ங ங

Try making the letter ங on your own.

Karidu the bear is only allowed to walk on stones that are marked ௫. He can only move between stones that touch each other. Can you find a way for Babu to reach his mother sleeping in the den?

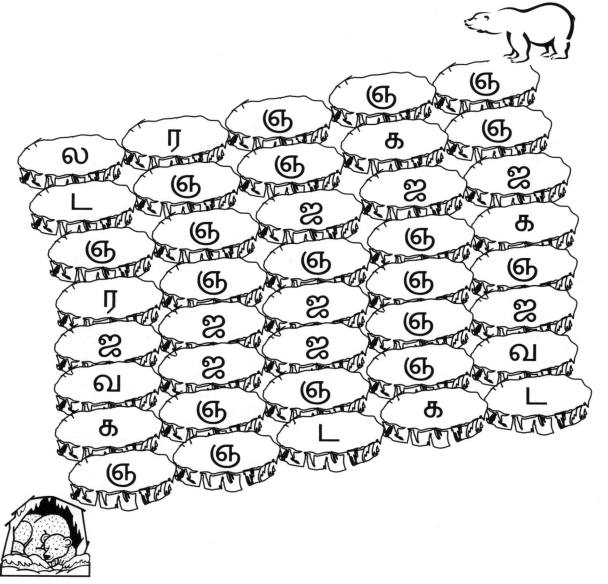

41

L

The Tamil letter L usually makes the sound of t in **tu**b. In some cases, it makes the sound of d in **du**b or th in fa**th**er.

Color me red

Color me green

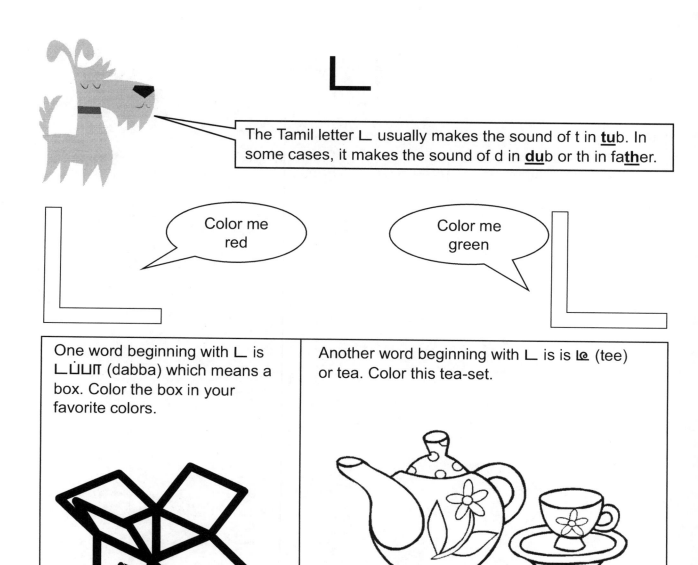

One word beginning with L is லூபா (dabba) which means a box. Color the box in your favorite colors.

Another word beginning with L is is டீ (tee) or tea. Color this tea-set.

Try making the letter L on your own.

⌐

Devika is tired and hungry after her dance and wants to eat something. But she can only walk on the stones marked ⌐ with her ornamnets. Can you find a way for Devika to reach a meal? What does she get to eat?

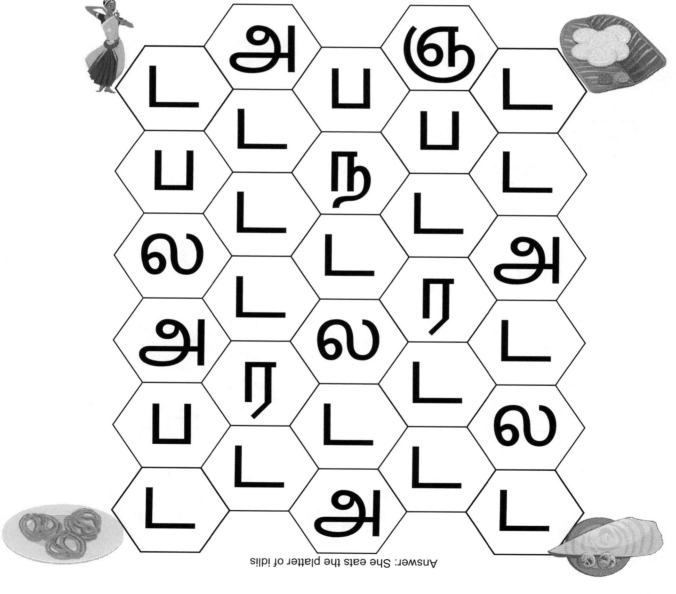

Answer: She eats the platter of idlis

ணா

The Tamil vowel ணா makes the sound of hard n in cra**n**k. It is usually found in the middle of the words.

Color me red

Color me green

One word containing ணா is கண்ணாடி (kannadi) or mirror. Color this mirror.

Another word containing ணா is வெண்ணெய் (vennai) or butter. Color this bar of butter.

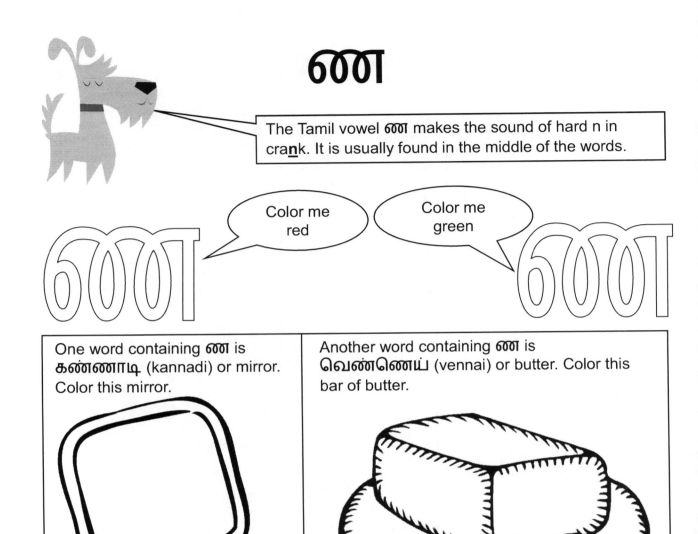

ணா ணா ணா ணா

Try making the letter ணா on your own.

ண

Santa knows that only the stockings marked with the letter ண belong to kids who have been nice. He will only fill those stockings with gifts. Can you color the stockings Santa will fill red?

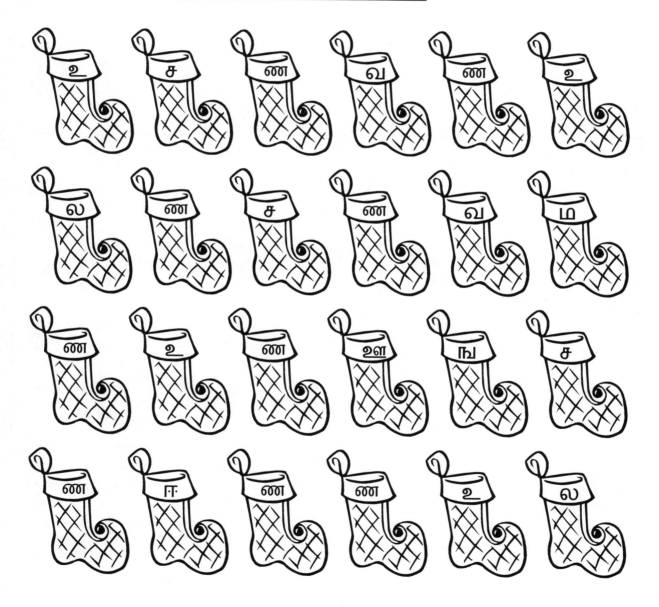

45

த

The Tamil letter த usually makes the sound of th in **th**ug. Sometimes, it makes the sound of dh in **dh**arma.

Color me red

Color me green

One word beginning with த is தயிர் (thayir) or yogurt. Color this yougurt container.

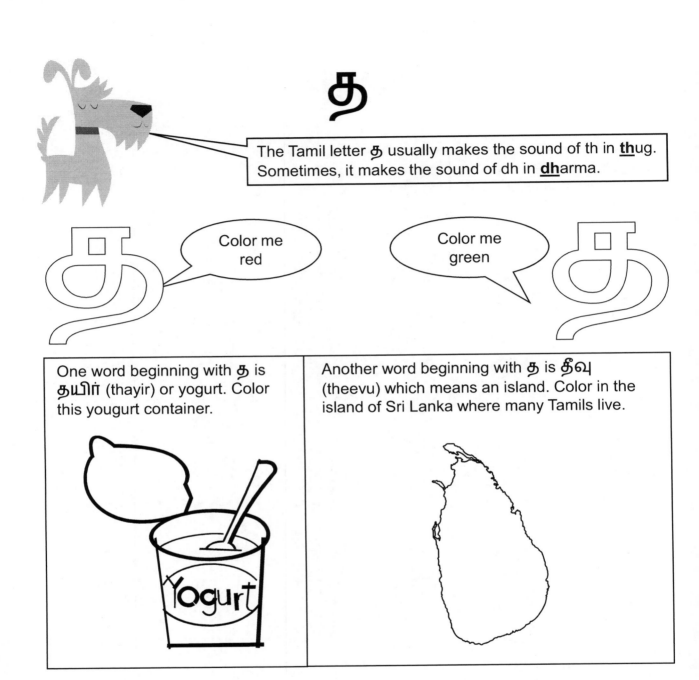

Another word beginning with த is தீவு (theevu) which means an island. Color in the island of Sri Lanka where many Tamils live.

Try making the letter த on your own.

த

Some of the apples on this page are of type த and others are of different types. Can you circle and color all the apples of type த?

ந

The Tamil letter ந makes the sound of n in **nu**rse.

Color me red

Color me green

One word beginning with ந is நாய் (naa-ai) or dog. Color this cute dog.

Another word beginning with ந is நரி (nari) or fox. Color this fox with the bushy tail.

Try making the letter ந on your own.

ந

Only some of the pictures shown here begin with ந .
Can you circle those pictures that begin with it?
Color those pictures green.

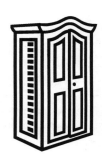

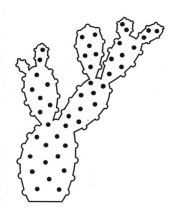

List of Words				
சாவி (saavi)	key		நாகம் (naagam)	Cobra
அலமாரி (alamaari)	cupboard		நாகதாளி (naagataali)	cactus
சிங்கம் (singam)	lion		நகம் (nagam)	nail

49

ப

The Tamil letter ப usually makes the sound of p in **p**up, but on occasions it makes the sound of b in **bu**s.

Color me red

Color me green

One word beginning with ப is படகு (padagu) or boat. Color this boat.

Another word beginning with ப is பசு (pasu) or cow. Color this cow.

Try making the letter ப on your own.

ப

Only some of the pictures shown here begin with ப .
Can you circle those pictures that begin with it?
Color those pictures green.

List of Words			
பரிசு (parisu)	prize	நாகம் (naagam)	Cobra
முயல் (muyal)	rabbit	பல்லி (palli)	lizard
தண்ணீர் (thanneer)	water	பஞ்சி (panji)	cotton

51

ம

The letter ம makes the sound of m in **m**uch.

Color me red

Color me green

One word beginning with ம is மரம் (maram) or wood. Color this pile of wood.

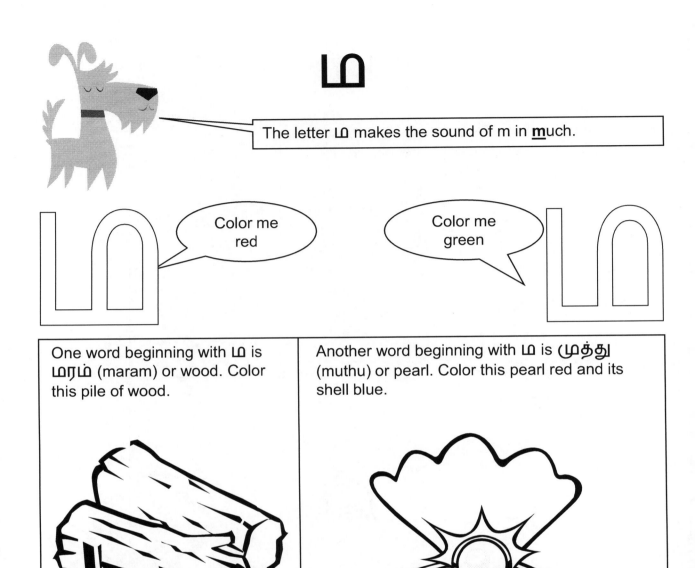

Another word beginning with ம is முத்து (muthu) or pearl. Color this pearl red and its shell blue.

Try making the letter ம on your own.

ம

Amit Rabbit is only allowed to hop onto adjacent letter stones that are marked ம. Find a way for Amit to reach a carrot. Color the stones Amit will jump on his way blue.

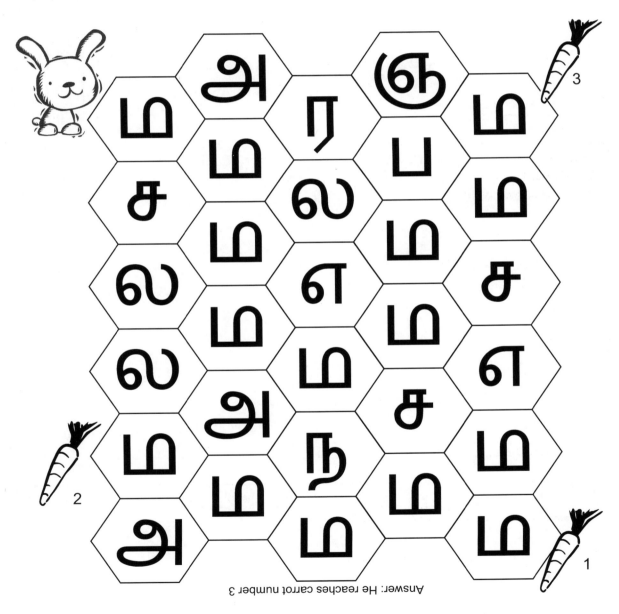

Answer: He reaches carrot number 3

ய

The letter ய makes the sound of ya in **ya**tch.

Color me red

Color me green

One word beginning with ய is யானை (yannai) or elephant. Color this elephant.

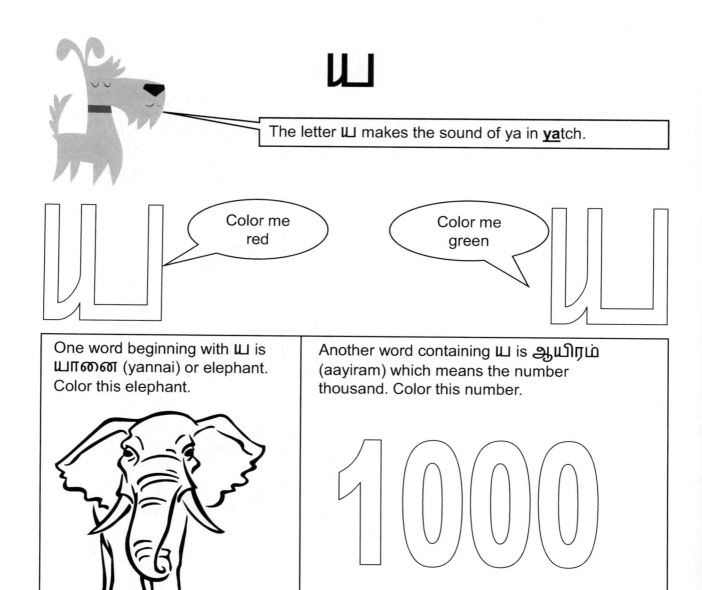

Another word containing ய is ஆயிரம் (aayiram) which means the number thousand. Color this number.

1000

Try making the letter ய on your own.

ய

My alphabet soup has quite a few letters and I have lost track of the number of ய in my soup. Can you find out how many ய are in my bowl of soup?

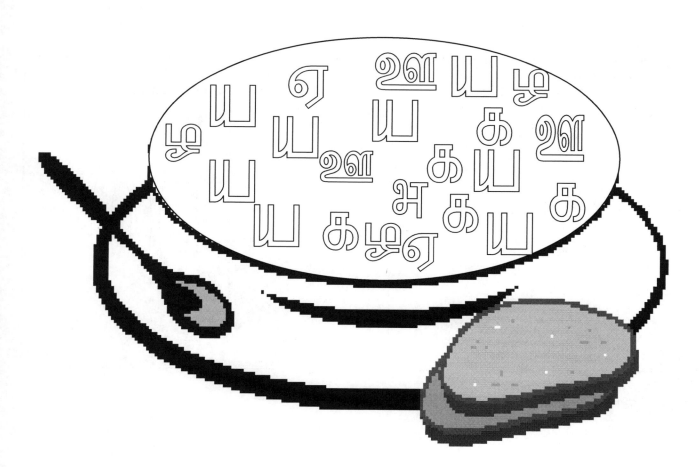

ற

The Tamil letter ற makes the sound of r in **ru**n.

ற Color me red

Color me green ற

One word beginning with ற is றாஜா (raja) or king. Color this king.

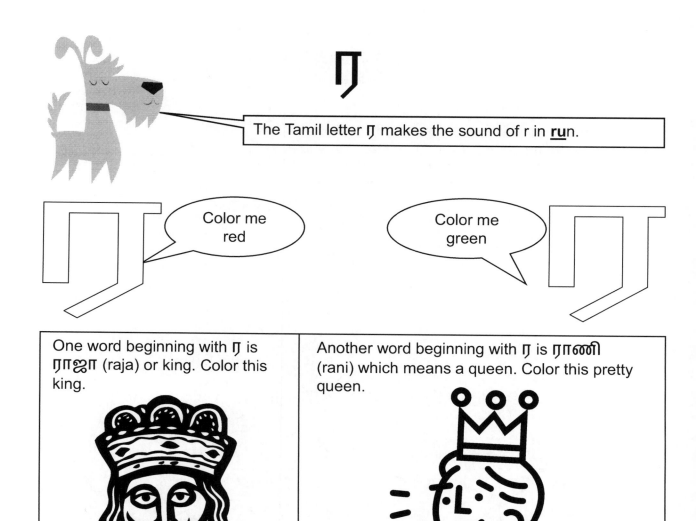

Another word beginning with ற is றாணி (rani) which means a queen. Color this pretty queen.

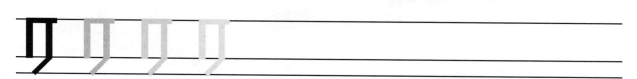

Try making the letter ற on your own.

ர

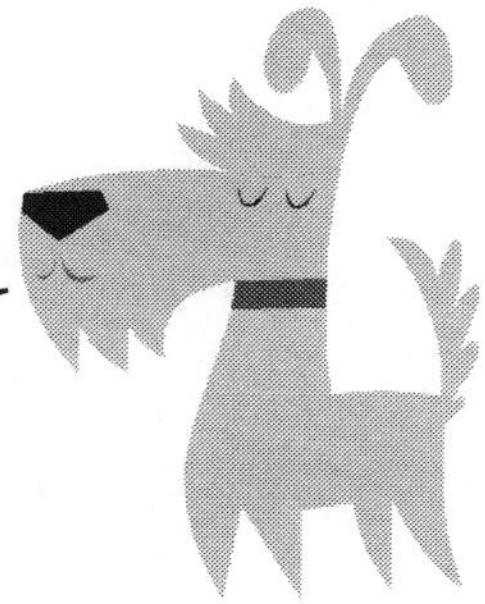

Only some of the pictures shown here begin with ர .
Can you circle those pictures that begin with it?

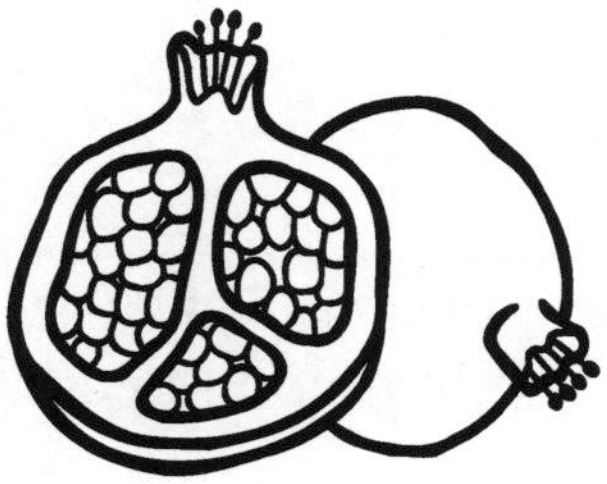
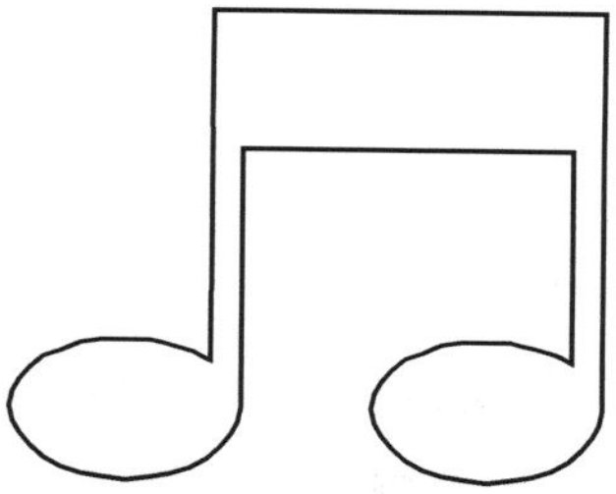
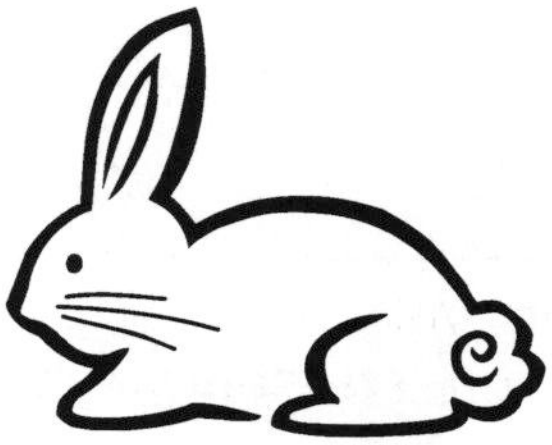

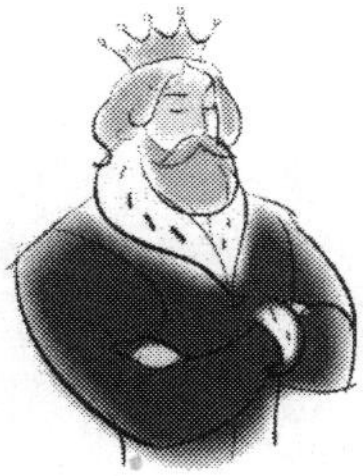
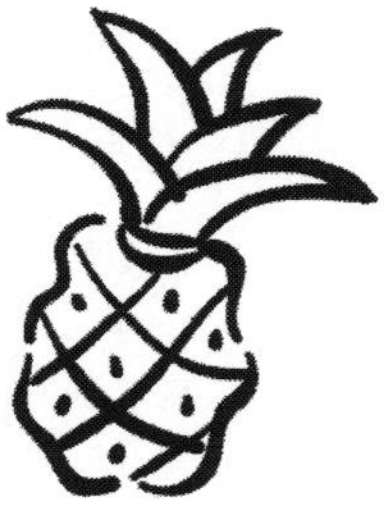
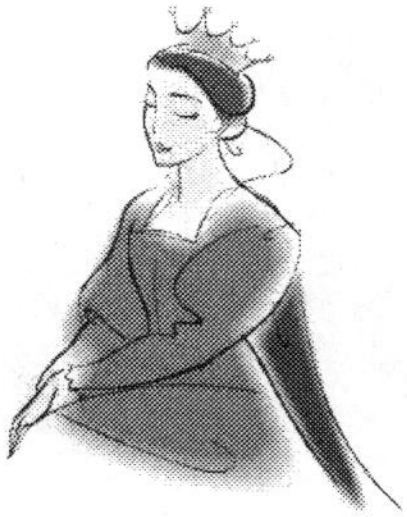

List of Words

மாதுளை (madulai)	pomegranate	ராகம் (raagam)	Musical note
முயல் (muyal)	rabbit	ராஜா (raja)	king
அனாசி (anasi)	pineapple	ராணி (rani)	queen

ல

The letter ல makes the sound of l in **lo**ve.

Color me red

Color me green

One word beginning with ல is லாடம் (ladam) or horse-shoe. Color this horse-shoe brown.

Another word beginning with ல is லட்சம் (laksam) which means one hundred thousand. Color this large number.

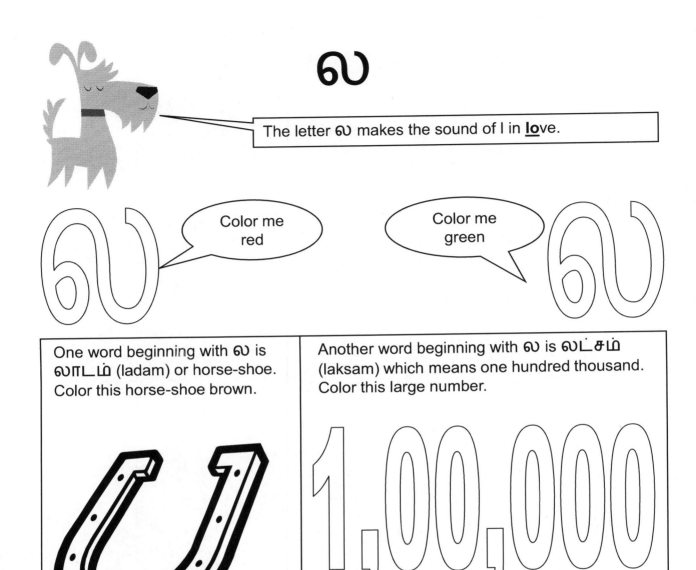

1,00,000

ல ல ல ல

Try making the letter ல on your own.

ல

Only some of the pictures shown here begin with ல.
Can you circle those pictures that begin with it?

List of Words			
லதி (lathi)	Staff/cane	சூரியன் (suriyan)	Sun
லக்ஷமி (lakshmi)	Goddess Laxmi	லாடம் (ladam)	horse-shoe
அனாசி (anasi)	pineapple	டீ (tea)	tea

வ

The Tamil letter வ is makes the sound of v in **vu**lture.

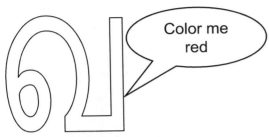

Color me red

Color me green

One word beginning with வ is வானம் (vaanam) or sky. Color the clouds in the sky.

Another word beginning with வ is வட்டம் (vattam) which means a circle. Color this circle in your favorite color.

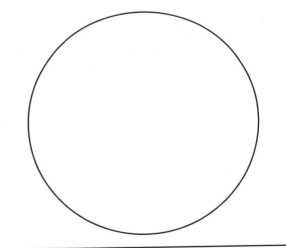

வ வ வ வ

Try making the letter வ on your own.

வ

Amit Rabbit is only allowed to hop onto adjacent letter stones marked வ. Find a way for Amit to reach a carrot. Color the stones Amit will jump on his way red.

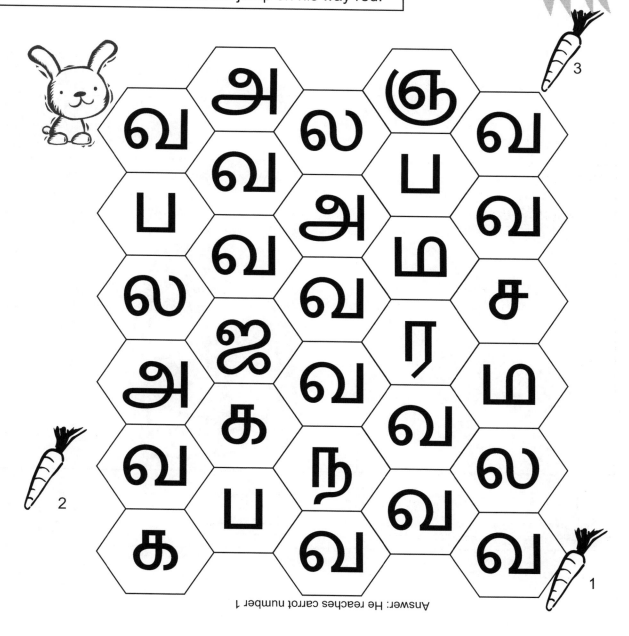

ழ

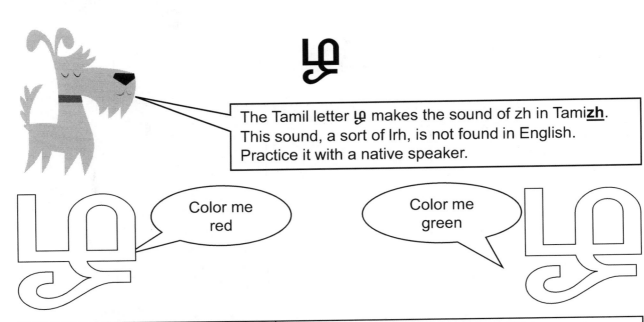

The Tamil letter ழ makes the sound of zh in Tami**zh**. This sound, a sort of Irh, is not found in English. Practice it with a native speaker.

Color me red

Color me green

One word containing ழ is கோழி (kozhi) or a chicken. Color this chicken.

Another word containing ழ is கீழ் (keezh) which means the direction East. Color this compass, circling out East in red and other directions in green.

ழ ழ ழ ழ

Try making the letter ழ on your own.

My alphabet soup has quite a few letters and I have lost track of the number of ழ in my soup. Can you find out how many ழ are in my bowl of soup?

Answer: There are eleven ழ in the soup.

ள

The Tamil letter **ள** makes the sound of ll as in fu**ll**.

Color me red

Color me green

One word containing **ள** is **வாளி** (vaalli) or a bucket. Color this bucket.

Another word containing **ள** is **நாகதாளி** (naagataali) which means a cactus. Color this cactus a desert green color.

Try making the letter **ள** on your own.

ள

Golu Elephant is only allowed to walk on boxes that are marked ள. He can only move between adjacent boxes left/right or up/down. Can you find a way for Golu to reach the bananas?

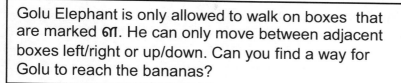

ள	ஈ	ல	வ	ஈ	வ	ஜ	வ	ஈ	வ	ர
ள	ஜ	ஈ	ல	ஈ	ஜ	ஈ	வ	வ	க	க
ள	ள	ள	ள	ள	ள	ள	ள	ள	க	ள
வ	ஈ	ஈ	ஈ	ஈ	ப	ள	ஈ	ஜ	ஜ	ள
ம	ப	இ	அ	இ	ர	ள	க	வ	ஈ	ள
ஈ	ள	ள	ள	ள	ள	ஈ	ள	ள	ள	ள
ந	ள	ஜ	வ	ப	ஈ	வ	ம	ள	ஈ	ள
ள	ள	ர	ஈ	ம	ஈ	வ	ஈ	ள	ஈ	ள
ஈ	ள	ள	ள	ள	ள	ள	ள	ள	ஜ	ள

65

ற

The Tamil letter ற makes the sound of rh as in **rh**inestone. No common words begin with it, but it is found in middle of many words.

Color me red

Color me green

One word containing ற is எறும்பு (erhumpu) or ant. Color this cute ant.

Another word containing ற is பறவை (parhavai) which is a bird. Color this bird.

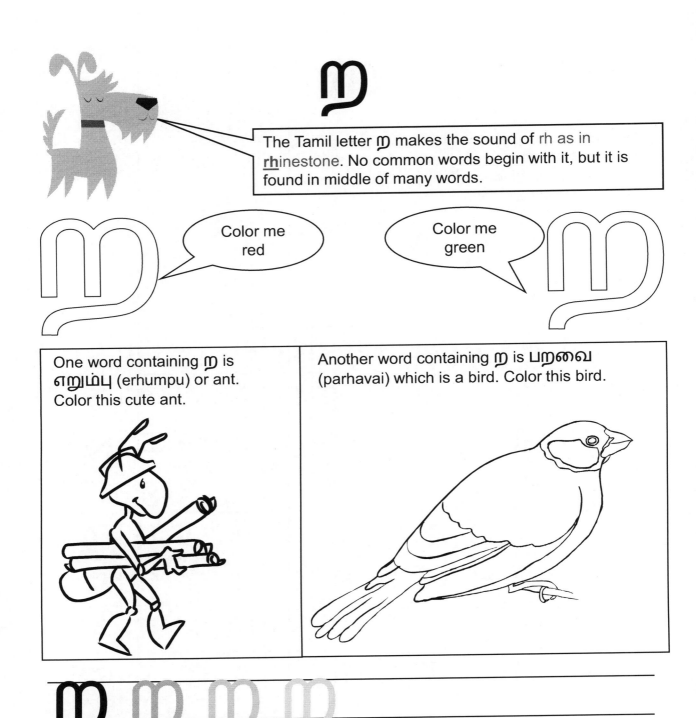

Try making the letter ற on your own.

My alphabet soup has quite a few letters and I have lost track of the number of ற in my soup. Can you find out how many ற are in my bowl of soup?

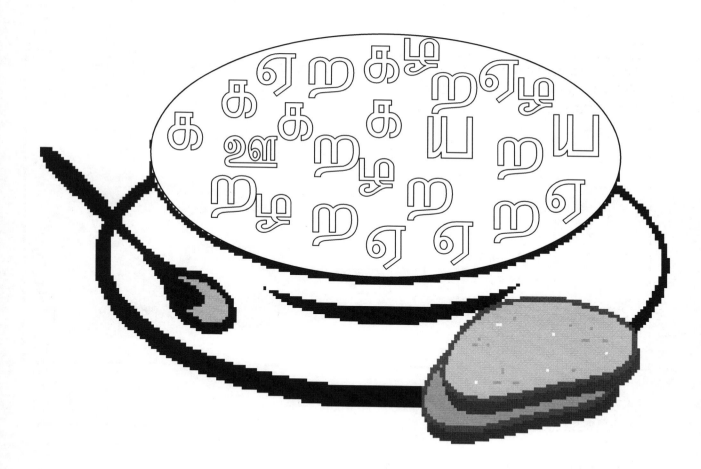

Answer: There are eight ற in the soup.

ன

The Tamil letter **ன** makes the sound of n as in stu**nn**ed.

Color me red

Color me green

One word containing **ன** is ஜன்னல் (jannal) or a window. Color this window and its curtains.

Another word containing **ன** is மீன் (meen) or a fish. Color this fish.

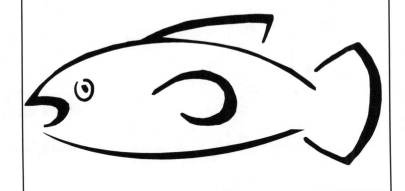

ன ன ன ன

Try making the letter **ன** on your own.

ன

Some of the apples on this page are of type ன and others are of different types. Can you circle and color all the apples of type ன?

The *grantha* letters are consonants that are borrowed from other languages to Tamil. They are used to write words originating from those languages.

One language that has donated many words to Tamil is Sanskrit. Grantha letters have sounds that are in Sanskrit, and were not in original Tamil.

Grantha Letters

ஜ ஷ ஸ ஹ க்ஷ

ஜ

The Tamil letter ஜ makes the sound of j in **ju**g.

Color me red

Color me green

One word containing ஜ is**மேஜை** (mejai) or table. Color this table.

Another word containing ஜ is புஜம் (bujam) which means the arm. Color this duo who are arm-wrestling.

ஜ   ஜ   ஜ   ஜ

Try making the letter ஜ on your own.

Jaju the Giraffe is only allowed to walk on stones that are marked ஐ. He can only move between stones that touch each other. Can you help Jaju reach his ship?

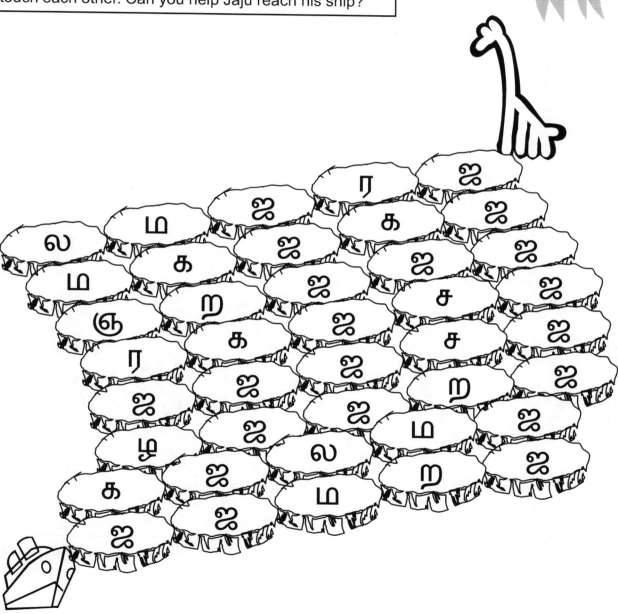

73

ஷ

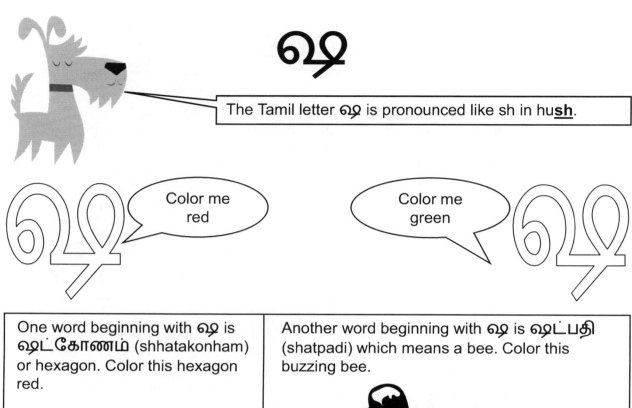

The Tamil letter ஷ is pronounced like sh in hu**sh**.

Color me red

Color me green

One word beginning with ஷ is ஷட்கோணம் (shhatakonham) or hexagon. Color this hexagon red.

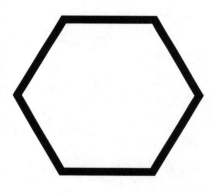

Another word beginning with ஷ is ஷட்பதி (shatpadi) which means a bee. Color this buzzing bee.

ஷ ஷ ஷ ஷ

Try making the letter ஷ on your own.

ஷ

My alphabet soup has quite a few letters and I have lost track of the number of ஷ in my soup. Can you find out how many ஷ are in my bowl of soup?

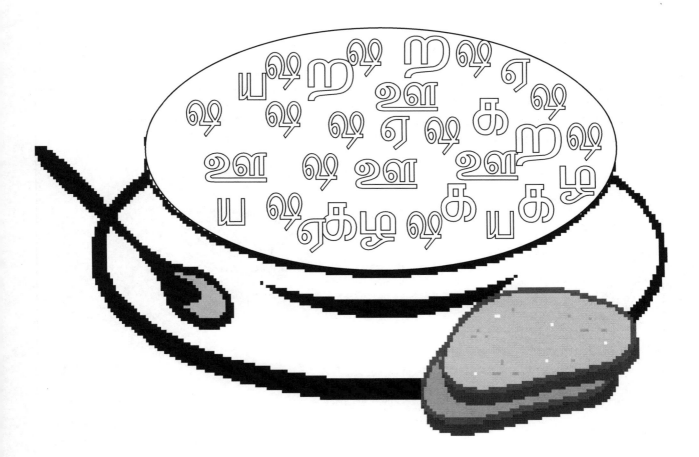

75

സ

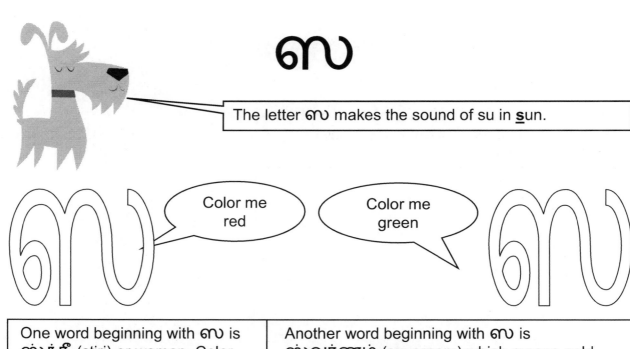

The letter സ makes the sound of su in **s**un.

Color me red

Color me green

One word beginning with സ is സ്ത്രീ (stiri) or woman. Color this woman and her clothes.

Another word beginning with സ is സ്വര്‍ണ്ണം (suvarnam) which means gold. Color the pot full of gold coins.

സ സ സ സ

Try making the letter സ on your own.

സ

Some of the toffees on this page are of type സ and others are of different types. Can you circle and color all the toffees of type സ.

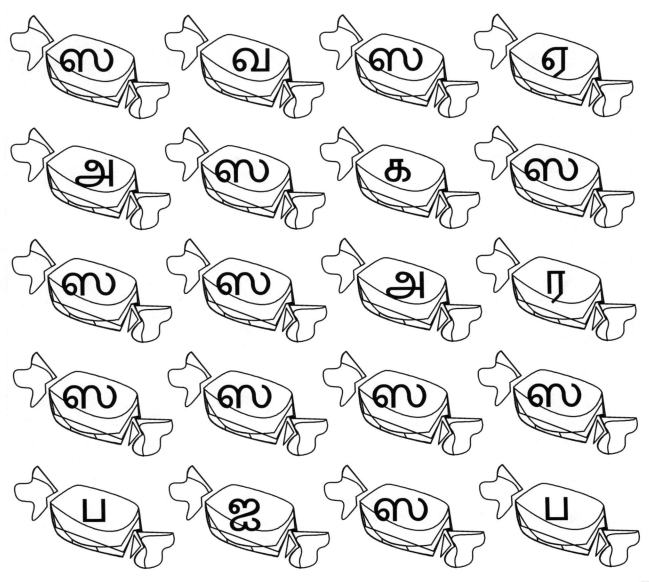

ஹ

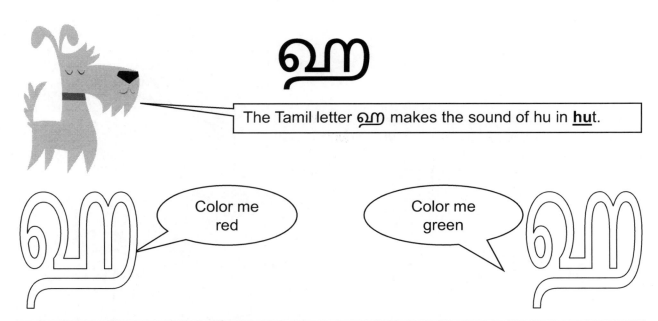

The Tamil letter ஹ makes the sound of hu in **hu**t.

Color me red

Color me green

One word beginning with ஹ is ஹஸ்தம் (hastam) or hand. Color these hands brown.

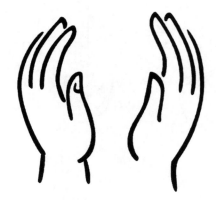

Another word beginning with ஹ is ஹஸ்தி (hasti) which means elephant. Color this elephant black.

Try making the letter ஹ on your own.

ஹ

Only some of the pictures shown here begin with ஹ.
Can you circle those pictures that begin with it?
Color those pictures green. Color the others red.

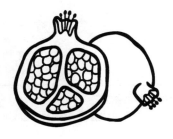

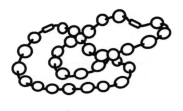

List of Words			
மாதுளை (matulari)	pomegranate	ஹஸ்தி (hasti)	elephant
மாலை (malai)	necklace	ஹஸ்தம் (hastam)	hand
வயிரம் (vayiram)	diamond	அனாசி (anaci)	pineapple

க்ஷ

The Tamil letter க்ஷ makes the sound of **ksh**.

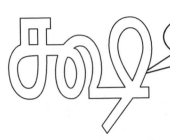

Color me red

Color me green

One word containing க்ஷ is டிக்ஷனரி (dictionary). Color this dictionary.

One word beginning with க்ஷ is க்ஷத்திரியன் (kshattriya) which means a warrior. Color this warrior.

க்ஷ க்ஷ க்ஷ க்ஷ

Try making the letter க்ஷ on your own.

சூழி

Some of the apples on this page are of type சூழி and others are of different types. Can you circle and color all the apples of type சூழி?

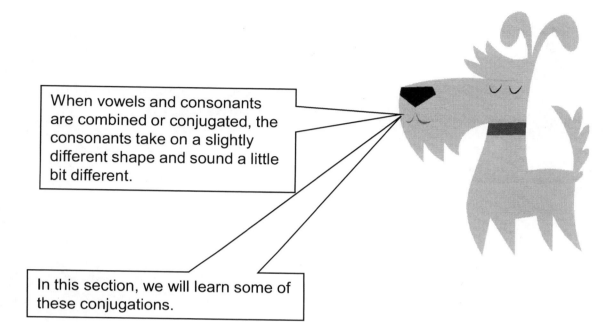

When vowels and consonants are combined or conjugated, the consonants take on a slightly different shape and sound a little bit different.

In this section, we will learn some of these conjugations.

Letter Combinations

When the consonants occur without any vowels accompanying them, they have a very short sound. In that case, the consonants have a small dot on top of them as shown below. The opposite page shows the normal form of consonants.

க் ங் ச்

ஞ் ட் ண்

த் ந் ப்

ம் ய் ர்

Notice how the form of **ர** has changed when it is without அ

ல் வ் ழ்

ள் ற் ன்

ஜ் ஷ் ஸ்

ஹ் ஃ ஷ்

அ

When the consonants team up with the vowel அ, the give up the dot on the top, and take their normal form and pronouncement. Then, they look like this.

க ங ச

ஞ ட ண

த ந ப

ம ய ர

ல வ ழ

ள ற ன

ஜ ஷ ஸ

ஹ க்ஷ

Isn't it good to have friends, and be able to make the normal sound!

Letter Combinations

Consonants and vowels combine like peanut butter and jelly to make different flavors of sounds. Here is what happens to shape and sounds when க் combines with the jelly of first six vowels.

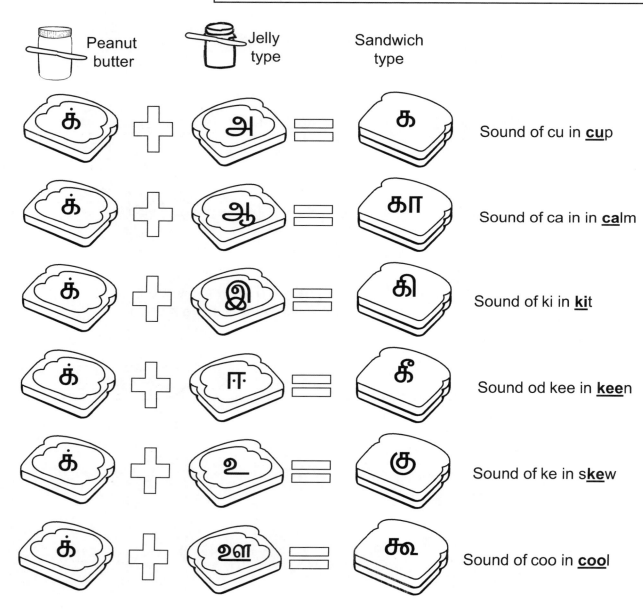

Peanut butter   Jelly type   Sandwich type

க் + அ = க   Sound of cu in **cu**p

க் + ஆ = கா   Sound of ca in in **ca**lm

க் + இ = கி   Sound of ki in **ki**t

க் + ஈ = கீ   Sound od kee in **kee**n

க் + உ = கு   Sound of ke in s**ke**w

க் + ஊ = கூ   Sound of coo in **coo**l

Letter Combinations

Here is the form and sound of க் when it combines with the last six vowels.

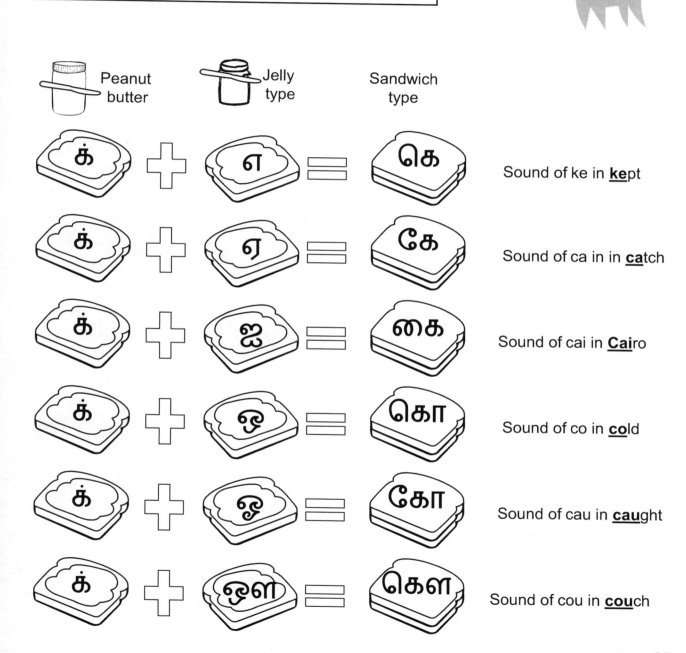

Peanut butter | Jelly type | Sandwich type

க் + எ = கெ   Sound of ke in **ke**pt

க் + ஏ = கே   Sound of ca in in **ca**tch

க் + ஐ = கை   Sound of cai in **Cai**ro

க் + ஒ = கொ   Sound of co in **co**ld

க் + ஓ = கோ   Sound of cau in **cau**ght

க் + ஔ = கௌ   Sound of cou in **cou**ch

ஆ

When the consonants combine with the vowel , they all add a long aa sound after themselves and take the forms shown on this page.

கா ஙா சா

ஞா டா ணா

தா நா பா

மா யா ரா

லா வா ழா

ளா றா னா

It is like going to the doctor's office and saying aah after each consonant.

ஜா ஷா ஸா

ஹா க்ஷா

Jaju the Giraffe is only allowed to walk on stones that touch each other and are marked with a letter conjugated with ஆ. Can you help Jaju reach his ship?

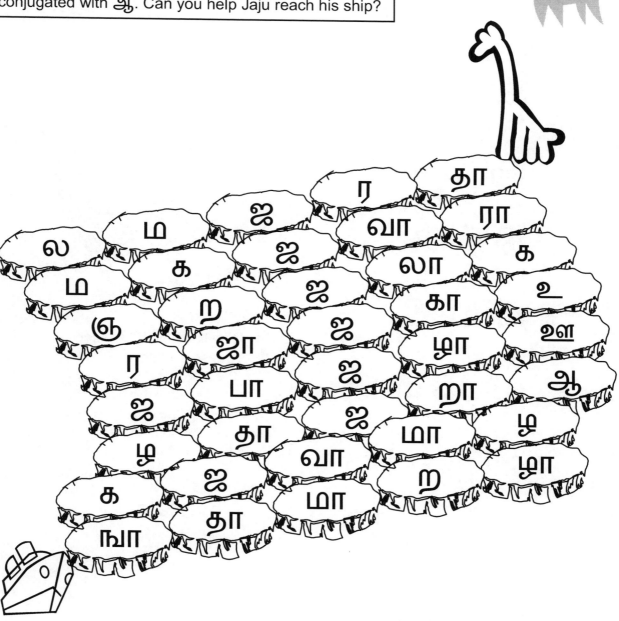

When the consonants team up with the vowel இ, they have the sound of short I added to them. Then they look like this.

கி ஙி சி

ஞி டி ணி

தி நி பி

மி யி ரி

லி வி ழி

ளி றி னி

ஜி ஷி ஸி

ஹி க்ஷி

The little line after each consonant shows that the vowel இ is coming along for the ride. Notice the change of shape in ㄲ and the location of the line in ㄴ.

Some of the apples on this page are marked with letters conjugated with இ. How many such apples are on the page.

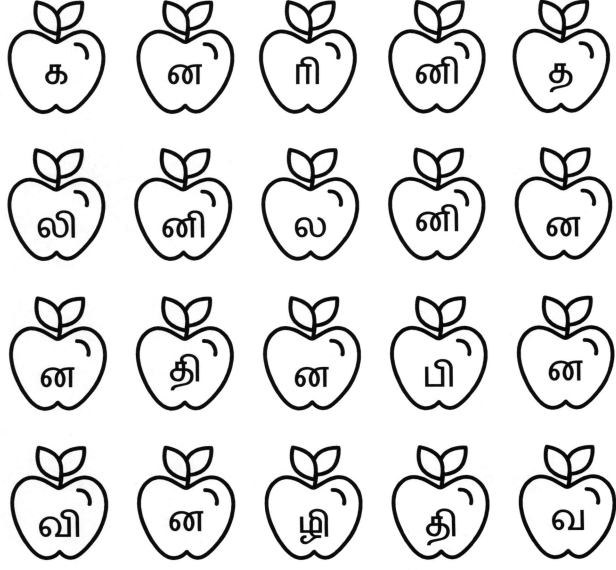

ஈ

When the consonants team up with the vowel ஈ, they have the sound of long ee added to them. Then they look like this.

கீ ஙீ சீ

ஞீ டீ ணீ

தீ நீ பீ

மீ யீ ரீ

லீ வீ ழீ

ளீ றீ னீ

ஜீ ஷீ ஸீ

ஹீ க்ஷீ

Notice the slightly different forms used for the letters ட and ற

92

ஈ

Some of the toffees on this page are marked with a vowel carrying a constant conjugated with ஈ. Can you circle and color all those toffees?

உ

When the consonants team up with the vowel உ, they have the sound of short u added to them. Then they look like this.

கு ஙு சு

ஞு டு ணு

து நு பு

மு யு ரு

லு வு ழு

ளு று னு

ஜு ஷு ஸு

ஹு க்ஷு

Notice that this vowel changes forms in different ways for different consonants.

உ

Amit Rabbit is only allowed to hop onto adjacent stones that are marked with a constant conjugated with உ . Find a way for Amit to reach a carrot? Color all the stones Amit will need to jump on his way blue.

	து	பு	த	
கு஁	வ	அ	லு	அ
ஜீ	அ	கு	த	
ல	உ	ர	ஞு	
ஹ	ர	ய	வு	
ப	த	நு	ஜீ	
து	ல	ஞு	து	
	அ			

உள

When the consonants team up with the vowel உள, they have the sound of long oo added to them. Then they look like:

கூ ஙூ தூ

ஞூ டூ ணூ

தூ நூ பூ

மூ யூ ரூ

லூ வூ ழூ

ளூ றூ னூ

ஜூ ஷூ ஸூ

ஹூ க்ஷூ

Notice that this vowel changes forms in different ways for different consonants.

ஊ

What will be the form on the sandwich when you combine different consonants with jelly type of ஊ. Write that form on the sandwich.

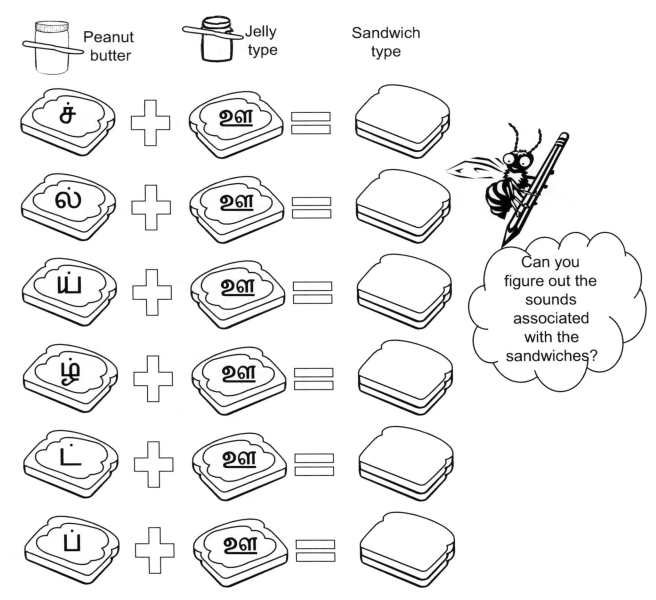

Peanut butter

Jelly type

Sandwich type

ச் + ஊ =

ல் + ஊ =

ய் + ஊ =

ழ் + ஊ =

ட் + ஊ =

ப் + ஊ =

Can you figure out the sounds associated with the sandwiches?

97

எ/ஏ

When the consonants team up with the vowel எ, they take the form shown on the left, and with the vowel ஏ, the form shown on the right.

எ	ஏ
கெ ஙெ செ	கே ஙே சே
ஞெ டெ ணெ	ஞே டே ணே
தெ நெ பெ	தே நே பே
மெ யெ ரெ	மே யே ரே
லெ வெ ழெ	லே வே ழே
ளெ றெ னெ	ளே றே னே
ஜெ ஷெ ஸெ	ஜே ஷே ஸே
ஹெ க்ஷெ	ஹே க்ஷே

எ/ஏ

Raman is collecting all letters on this page that are conjugated with vowel of and Mohan is collecting the ones conjugated with. The one with more letters wins. Who will win the contest?

கெ	லே	ச	யே	டெ	ம
ப	ரெ	ன	ஜெ	ஷ	யே
ங	ளே	றே	ணெ	ங	ஸ
த	ஜே	த	ஹ	வே	ய
பெ	நே	ழே	ன	கெ	ஜ
கெ	கி	கா	கே	கோ	கெள
வே	த	ப	ழே	னெ	ண
தோ	கெள	பா	ரா	தி	ஜூ
மெ	ழ	ஜ	ரே	ஷெ	ஹ
கா	தி	சு	லே	வ	ஷ
பே	வ	ளே	ஜ	யே	தெ

ஐ/ஒ

When the consonants team up with the vowel ஐ, they take the form shown on the left, and with the vowel ஒ, the form shown on the right.

ஐ

கை நைங சை

நைஞ டை ணை

தை நை பை

மை யை ரை

லை வை ழை

ளை றை னை

ஜை ஷை ஸை

ஹை க்ஷை

ஒ

கொ ஙொ சொ

ஞொ டொ ணொ

தொ நொ பொ

மொ யொ ரொ

லொ வொ ஷொ

ளொ றொ னொ

ஜொ ஷொ ஸொ

ஹொ க்ஷொ

ஐ/ஒ

What will be the form on the sandwich when you combine different consonants with jelly type of ஐ/ஒ.

Write that form on the sandwich.

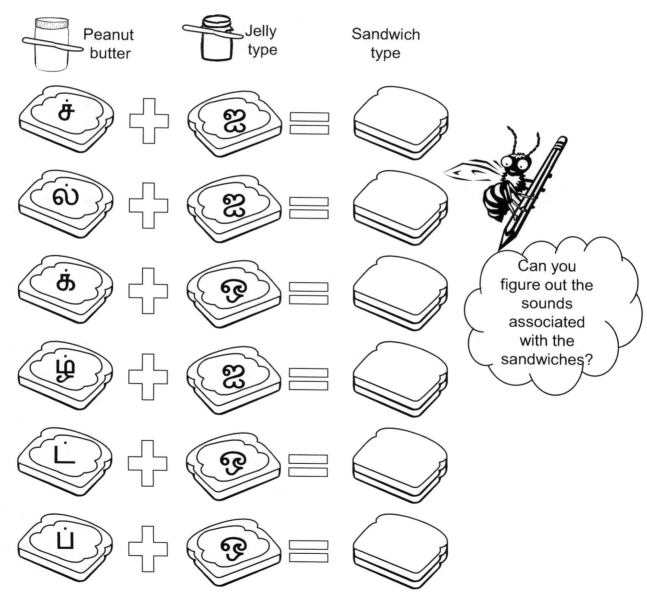

Peanut butter

Jelly type

Sandwich type

ச் + ஐ =

ல் + ஐ =

க் + ஒ =

ழ் + ஐ =

ட் + ஒ =

ப் + ஒ =

Can you figure out the sounds associated with the sandwiches?

கோ நோ சோ

ஞோ டோ ணோ

தோ நோ போ

மோ யோ ரோ

லோ வோ ழோ

ளோ றோ னோ

ஜோ ஷோ ஸோ

ஹோ க்ஷோ

Some of the apples on this page are marked with a vowel carrying a constant conjugated with ஒ. Can you circle and color all those apples?

ஒள

When the consonants team up with the vowel ஒள, they have the sound of ow added to them. Then they look like this.

கௌ ஙௌ சௌ

ஞௌ டௌ ணௌ

தௌ நௌ பௌ

மௌ யௌ ரௌ

லௌ வௌ ழௌ

ளௌ றௌ னௌ

ஜௌ ஷௌ ஸௌ

ஹௌ க்ஷௌ

ஒள

Some of the toffees on this page are marked with a vowel carrying a constant conjugated with ஒள. Can you circle and color all those toffees?

ஸா வெள ஸோ ஏ

நோ ஸ கோ ஸ

ஸ ஸ ஜோ ர

தெள போ ஸ ஸ

போ ஞோ ஸ வெ

Letter Combinations

Make your own peanut butter and jelly sandwiches with Tamil consonants and vowels.

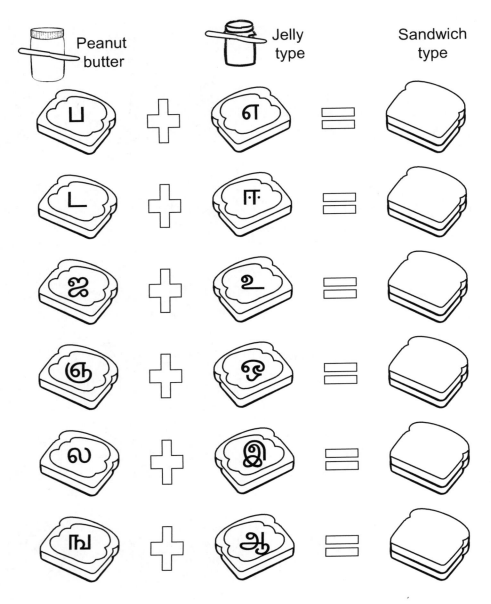

Peanut butter   Jelly type   Sandwich type

ப + எ =

ட + ஈ =

ஃ + உ =

கு + ஒ =

ல + இ =

ங + ஆ =

Letter Combinations

Make your own peanut butter and jelly sandwiches with Tamil consonants and vowels.

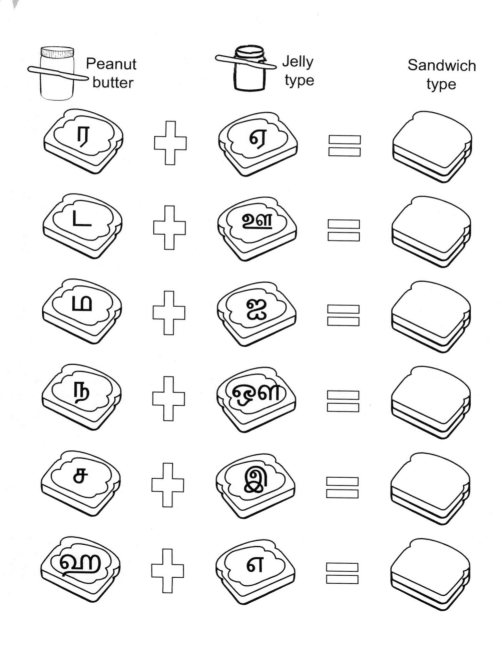

Chanda Books Publications

Level 1 Hindi:

- Aamoo the Aam
- Aamoo the Aam – Part II
- Aamoo the Aam – Part III
- Hindi Children's Book Level 1 Easy Reader

Level 2 Hindi:

- Tara Sitara
- Tara ke Kisse
- Hindi Children's Book Level 2 Easy Reader

Level 3 Hindi:

- Sonu ke kisse
- Sonu ke Afsane
- Sonu ke Tyohar
- Hindi Children's Book Level 3 Easy Reader
- Hindi Nursery Rhymes

Alphabet Books:

- Bengali Alphabet Book
- Gujarati Alphabet Book
- Hindi Alphabet Book
- Marathi Alphabet Book
- Punjabi Alphabet Book
- Tamil Alphabet Book

Hindi Activity Books:

- Learn Hindi Alphabet Activity Workbook
- Learn Hindi Writing Activity Workbook
- Learn Hindi Matras Activity Workbook
- Learn Hindi Vocabulary Activity Workbook
- Learn Hindi Grammar Activity Workbook
- Hindi Activity Workbook

Bengali Activity Books:

- Learn Bengali Alphabet Activity Workbook
- Learn Bengali Writing Activity Workbook
- Learn Bengali Vocabulary Activity Workbook

Punjabi Activity Books:

- Learn Punjabi Alphabet Activity Workbook
- Learn Punjabi Writing Activity Workbook
- Learn Punjabi Vocabulary Activity Workbook

Indian Culture Activity Books:

- Hinduism for Children Activity Workbook
- Indian Festivals Activity Workbook

Other Subjects:

- Bhajan Ganga
- Indian Culture Stories: Sanskar
- South Asian Immigration Stories

Tamil Activity Books:

- Learn Tamil Alphabet Activity Workbook
- Learn Tamil Writing Activity Workbook
- Learn Tamil Vocabulary Activity Workbook

Made in the USA
Middletown, DE
13 August 2017